Where I Go
(I Go Alone)

Fany Aktinol

Where I Go
(I Go Alone)

Translated by Jordan B. Jones

KBR
Greenville
2019

CONTENTS

Preface   11
Body   15
Fertility   16
The Keys to the House   17
Return   18
What Has Become of My Life   19
I Bend to the Wind   20
Autumns   21
We'd Always Get Lost   22
Inside Nature   23
Happiness   24
Moss on the Stone   25
Attachment   27
The Child I Am   29
From the Clay   31
The Sublime Moment   32
We Had Yet to Travel.   32
Take Flight   33
Delicate Crystal   35
Crossing   37
Reconciled   38
The Voice   40
Without Vanities   41
Flow   42
Light   43
Beyond the Border   44
Dive   45
North   47
The Same   48

Little Deity 49
Melinda's Secret 50
Our Farm 51
Caresses 52
May You Be Welcome 53
Drowning 54
Ocean of Time 55
Rest 56
Utopia 57
Mirage 58
Catharsis 59
Maturing 60
Love 61
Imminence 62
Elegy 63
Crack in the Soul 64
Ed 65
California, Summer 2012 66
The Mother 67
Legacy 68
Final Destination 69
Love Waits 70
Absence 71
Navigating 72
Tannenbaum 73
Matter of Life 74
Refuge 75
Sediments 77
The Days 78
The Rabbis Sing 80
Memories 81
Requiem 83

Shortcut	84
Allotted to Us Now.	84
To Whom?	85
At A Gallop	87
I	89
Sprouting	90
Disposable	91
Gravestone	92
Psalm	93
Festival of Lights	94
The Neighbor	96
Lap	97
Fall	98
The Unknown	99
Except for Me	100
Imponderable	101
Future	102
Sandy Hook	103
A Prayer	105
Thin Shell	106
Like the Diamond	107
Fragments	108
Scar	109
Canticle	110
Strand of Life	111
Mercy	113
Extemporaneous	115
Perception	116
Ancestrality	117
Sower of the Universe	118

I have no money, no resources, no hopes. I am
the happiest man alive. A year ago, six months ago,
I thought that I was an artist. I no longer think
about it, I am. Everything that was literature has
fallen from me. There are no more books to be
written, thank God.

Henry Miller, *Tropic of Cancer*

PREFACE

The atmosphere generated by the reading of Where I Go (I Go Alone) promotes communion between the delicacy of form and an unsettling symbolic density. The poetics of Fany Aktinol, in this her fifth book, present us with fragments of stories yet to be revealed, like enigmas which after each response rebound incessantly into new queries: "I will show the tender creature / My dreams and my fruits. / Everything I will leave as an inheritance. / Oh, pythoness, / How many enigmas there are to decipher in a life!" — fragment of the poem "From the Clay."

Fany, also a novelist, maintains this atmosphere throughout the entire book, offering us poetry seasoned generously with mystery. She submits her ellipses to the reader's imagination, in keeping with what Clarice Lispector suggests, in this quotation and in each rare exercise of her own poetic prose: "If you're going to write, at least be sure not to crush the between-the-lines with words."

Her lyricism sets the tone and gives unity to the work—not a tearful tone, but one of lean subjectivity, in which the poetic self exposes itself with courageous and lucid vulnerability: "Protect me, God, from the frozen earth / From the ground scorched by the sun. / From the bread that I once lacked / And that now runneth o'er" — excerpt from the poem "The Child I Am." And, in the beautiful lines of condensed bitterness of the poem "The Voice," a similar atmosphere: "I am like the cactus in a barren land, / The creeping vegetation of ruins. / The liquid I drink has the bitter taste / Of sour wine." But the poet also reveals to us an escape from the intimate cloister. In the encounter with the other we find the key; in love, the leap: "The secret gesture of tenderness, / Which I learned not to rely on, / Is enough to burst the dike / Of what I dam up inside" — in "Utopia."

In the lines of the poem "A Plea," Fany Aktinol brings us her origin and tradition, and the ancestral pain generated by war. This is the pain of wars that, violating geographical, temporal, and consanguineal boundaries, becomes the terrible legacy of all humanity: "Jerusalem, give us peace, / Save us from war, / Hear the prayers / Of those who depart, of those who stay. / Suffering is a twisted circle. [...] Hear the messages that choke / Each crack in the Wailing Wall / And that, murmured, saturate the atmosphere / From dawn to dusk / In a millenarian movement."

Fany's poetry is like a melodious whisper in which the words in our ears lead us to a tragedy wrapped in sweetness. The books proceeds in this tone, in which we see love and separation, time and distance, death and human vulnerability, nature, religiosity, guilt, and family—a theme which, in the poem "Attachment," hints at a reunion with a distant mother: "At the entrance of the village / They'd whispered to me / An old lady lives in the house / Almost without memory, with a far-off look. / Her children have long since left / Taking with them her life's true meaning."

Poignantly, the poem presents us with a characteristic of Fany's writing that makes narrative tangential (shown in this and in other sections of the book) without compromising the cadence or the rhythmic quality of the lines. On the contrary, they come to us as the characteristics and style of the writer who, throughout the book, tells us multifaceted stories in a melancholy tone, but not without hope. In writing, the poet finds identity, calm, support, and escape: "To write is to drink of spring water. / Soothe the distressed spirit and / with a bare breast receive the cold wind. / It is to find oneself on the way home. / To recognize oneself in the arrow shot forth" — from the poem "The Mother."

In *Where I Go (I Go Alone)*, a book of few rhymes and original metaphors, the author deceives herself if she believes in the message the title contains, since, wherever she goes, the ambitious reader will accompany her.

Carmen Moreno
(poet and fictionist)

BODY

I took form
Like the shapely olive tree of the plain.
I grew like the palm tree
And the plants of Jericho.

Those were happy times:
I bathed my surroundings
In jasmine and amber fragrance.
With myrrh I released a silky scent.
My dwelling was perfumed,
All cleansed and colored
By the tones of nature,
Tall and elevated.

My happiness made me so ethereal
That I seduced you no more.

FERTILITY

To me,
To accompany me
From the deep sky,
The dust of the sun, of the stars, and
The wind infusing the spirit of time
All life long.

To you,
The seed
Passed from generation to generation,
The fertile and watered valley.

On the threshold of the front gate
With bare feet,
I tread the rocky path through the grass
Bathed in smooth clarity.

All darkness has disappeared.
The plants and flowers have multiplied
In the garden garnished by small pebbles.

Everything bore fruit
And there's one who'll keep them.

THE KEYS TO THE HOUSE

To whom will I give
The keys to the house,
Overlaid with tender words
That flood the heart?

In the passage of this precious symbol
Strains of immense joy will sound
And some of torment,
The melodies will reflect the complete life.

Who will entrust the Word to me
Before this page is erased?

My garden was always
Blanketed with fruitful trees.
I never needed to care for it.

To whom will I give
The keys to the house
So warm and airy
With orchards to the south
And majestic mountains to the north?

Who will come to me
To receive a key
Sprayed with tears and longing?

RETURN

When you took my flowered spring
Far beyond the imaginary circle
That I drew at my feet
You also took my blood
That flowed through crimson flowers
And colored the boredom of unending afternoons.

You doubted whether I could esteem so much beauty.
But the sun continued to shine on my days
Illuminating the way
To the hidden fortress guarded by tall towers.

I multiplied myself,
I was instilled with immense courage
Near the abyss that pushed me
Close to God in the firmament.

A river of clear and gentle waters
Passed before me. Its invitation was subtle.
I bathed in it and cleansed myself of all impurities.
All that had once belonged to me,
Returned to my core.

WHAT HAS BECOME OF MY LIFE

It will happen on a night
In which you awaken with eyes open
To the darkness of the room.
To your remembrance will come
A verse which says
Eyes that give birth to tears.
Or:
Reap now the memories
Within your reach before they evaporate.
Everything will seem a remote dream,
To which you will pay no heed.

In some distant place
My children sleep.
I know not what they think
Or what fills their dreams.
But may they only be happy
And sleep the sleep of righteous men.
There is no need to worry
About what has become of my life.

Fany Aktinol

I BEND TO THE WIND

When you come for me,
With your spirit open to dialogue,
I rejoice in myself,
And I let myself be captured,
I bend to the wind
Like the tender plant.

You have an art with the word:
That which seems
To contain the world and time.

In my fragility,
After the instant of illumination
Comes the trance, the feeling of unbelonging,
And because I lack the power of enchantment,
I am fatally plummeting
Out of the universe,
Of space,
Weeping inside
With my soul in deep unrest,
In forgetfulness, in un-encounters.

Without you, I feel the singular horror
Of being always
Outside of the world that spins
And of the curve of time.

AUTUMNS

I enter the house
Shrouded in shadow.
I remove the dust that's gathered
Infiltrated
Through microscopic fissures
Invisible to the naked eye
During the autumns
When trees shake
And leaves fall.

Behind this movement
I decipher the message:
The most important attribute
Of the solitary, revelatory
Encounter—
I discover that under the dust
There is an unexpected glimmer
Reflecting my astonishment—
Under the dust
I hide myself.

WE'D ALWAYS GET LOST

In a remote past—
Before we were even born—
We moved through waste places.

We smoldered in the vastness of the deserts
And their extreme temperatures.
We braved the hostile harshness
Of the humid, dense forests.

We'd always get lost
Because we couldn't see the horizon.
The infinite space would catch fire
In our finite bodies.

Boundless nature,
The fury of its elements,
Unaware of its power,
Sparked in us
A stunning vulnerability.

We lost our way home.
We were alone—
We would burn by day
And sob by night.

INSIDE NATURE

Life is born each day.
This sun that shines,
This earth that overflows with light,
God conceived them today:
In the shimmer of our home's wall,
In the twinkling reflections on the floor,
In our open windows,
Where we can no longer discern its contours.

The light and the heat spread out
Around the table placed in the field
And the bed made up in a corner of the meadow.
Our house has no more walls—
We find ourselves inside nature—
Where flows pure gold
And from this spring we drink:
Of life, vast and resplendent.

HAPPINESS

From the summit
Falls the purple
Sunset
Touched by its own diaphanous substance
Staining it blood red.

The trees
Assume a hint of scarlet
The grass
Perfumes the air with its humid, penetrating
Greenness.
The place is familiar
But twilight has a way of enthralling,
Of turning an instant into something monumental.

The day prolongs itself beyond its bounds,
To the highest and most unfathomable
Time is steeped in eternity.
I let the twilight envelop me.
In this moment I am happy
Like a creature
Recreated at random
Not far from God.

MOSS ON THE STONE

Over substantial, voluminous
Stones
We felt on our soft skin
Like the moss from the earth
The days' design
On the house of solid walls
Immutable square dwellings
Half-closed
Constructed since time immemorial:
Without knowing we witnessed
A biblical time
Granted at an improper time.

The prelude was a speechless mouth.
The words' flight
Materialized in
colored, winged insects.
Flowers in the field
Absorbed the humidity
And brought tenderness to the heart.

Your steady hand
An extension of your body,
Loving and attentive,
Waved,
Inviting me to the exchange
As one who sows seeds in the earth.
I alone did not understand.

In the violet twilight

Surrounded by detached words
And indistinguishable sounds
You had a phosphorescent glow,
Everything emanated and bubbled
While I eluded myself
Turning myself invisible in the darkness
In a slow withering away.

ATTACHMENT

At the entrance of the village
They'd whispered to me
An old lady lives in the house
Almost without memory, with a far-off look.
Her children have long since left
Taking with them her life's true meaning.

I go looking for the house,
Of which I nurture profound remembrances,
With feelings so intense
They paralyze my reflexes.

I arrive at my destination:
An abandoned place, a lockless door.
Instinctively, I turn the knob and enter.
Despite my insecure steps, somewhat noisy,
On the floor of peeling wood,
Silence prevails.

In my despair I let out a suppressed cry:
"Mother, are you here?"
A movement of someone turning over in bed
Sharpens my ears.
I follow the sound, emotion gushing from my pores.
I am near collapse.

I know that nothing returns.
But I saw her, hugged her,
Kissed her face
When our tears mixed together

In the place where I was once happy
And where I cried again and again

Am I the one who waits
Or the one who now arrives?

THE CHILD I AM

Protect me, God, from the frozen earth
From the ground scorched by the sun.
From the bread that I once lacked
And that now runneth o'er.
Help me discern
Reality from utopia.
Save me from the terrible thoughts
That plague me—
And may I never act on them.

For, you took from me
The purest childhood possible.
And when I had just begun
To accept this hand dealt by fate,
A young mother
Was ripped from me.

So I placed myself before the world
Disoriented, like a dog without an owner.
Secretly I shed
Bloody tears
I innocently accepted
Without offering opinions or complaints,
Every good and every evil.

Because the days pass by unnoticed
I learned to wait silently
For the child that never comes.

And I, I will deliver
A son who will be my grandson.

FROM THE CLAY

The barren earth
Will be dunged and watered by me,
Transformed into a great orchard
With green, Sicilian citrus fruit,
Pomegranates and dates sweet as honey,
As abundant as the sensory journeys
Were infinite
In the dreams in which I passed through paradise.

I will cover my body
With the snowy whiteness of the last remaining
garment.
A sacred robe of pure linen
Reflecting sensibility and unfamiliarity
Because I have always been shaped this way,
With skepticism and the ancient clay
With which the rabbi of Prague created the golem,
That yearns in us through the centuries.

I do not wish to depart
Without knowing his face
I shall know, one day
If the seeds I scattered will bear fruit
If all the blood that pulsed
Through my body's arteries
Will be transformed into posterity.

I shall show the tender creature
My dreams and my fruits.
Everything I will leave as an inheritance.
Oh, pythoness,
How many enigmas there are to decipher in a life!

THE SUBLIME MOMENT

We went down along the path
After a long journey,
Exhausted and thirsty.
I brought lilies in my blistered hand…
We went down the way Absalom went down to Jericho
Along the Jordan valley.

Afternoon fell on a summer day.
The immense sky was so close
That I was saddened
By the lateness of the hour.
The flowers exhaled
An intoxicating aroma.
We sat on a bench of stone
So the sublime moment
Would not pass us by.
There, stone-like, we watched
The death of one more day and
The arrival of the silvery night
In an irreversible sequence.

And I waxed confident
When I saw the moon
Illuminating the path
We had yet to travel.

TAKE FLIGHT

The Mediterranean city
Had become rich and populous.
My time had come.
At the time of celebration
I left without saying goodbye.
I rode southward
Toward the desert
On the way to Petra—
The pink city
That stunned me with its brilliance.

Step by step I proceeded,
Spurred on by extremes.
I lay down to the sea
Of green and shimmering waters.
With fishes leaping around me
I sailed and sailed.
The algae became my ocean bed.

I climbed the tallest mountains.
I spent years of my life
In these climbs,
In the slow journey toward the top of the world
Where, exhausted, I arrived.

I walked barefoot in the desert
And shared my water with my horse.
Lightyears away from Petra or Jerusalem
I rode on the sandy beach
Along the entire length of the salty water
The glimmer of the horizon carved in my breast.

Fany Aktinol

I lived until the 21st century
With my porous memory
That is history and mirage
Taking turns.
I follow the path of the stones.
I see the future before me.
It's time to take flight.

DELICATE CRYSTAL

The golden afternoon
Resists awhile
So our eyes can see:
The man enveloped in fine mist
Who approaches:
He who knows his origins,
Bows down to the earth,
And looks as if he's been in Paradise.

It could be the prophet Eliyahu,
The Baal Shem Tov,
The mystic who invokes
The justice of the heavens
From the depths of the pit.

There is no forgetting,
Only memory,
This delicate crystal.

I was Moses,
He who did not enter the Promised Land,
But heard the voice of God on the mountain
And brought it, etched in stone
To deliver it to his people—
The Hebrew people who walked
Forty years in the desert
Without ever knowing peace.

In Jerusalem
Protecting the Temple

A wondrous marble lion
Reflects the golden light, eternal symbol
Of two millennia of exile.

CROSSING

The flame burns within
Consumes itself in rarified oxygen
On the feathery earth where I carefully tread.

Dreams and nightmares alternate
While the sky with cotton clouds
Protects me from falling into the abyss.

No one visits me
I am an exposed wire.
I squeeze the pain
Until it fits inside my body.

Soon I will cross an ocean
I will reach the other end of the rainbow
And gather fruits of all the colors of the universe.

RECONCILED

With an escapist vision,
The work constructed now on stone,
Now on sand,
The past of transgressors,
Foolish epics,
Has never come to me lightly.

And yet, the breath of life keeps me upright.
It pushes me to an unknown spatial geometry—
No place resembles this one—
I am strangely at peace
I float in a dreamlike state
Toward the setting sun.

In a rare burst
Of tenderness and lyricism
I feel nourished
By the inebriating atmosphere,
By the impalpable, elusive
Moment,
By the intense glow
And the infinity of colors
That tinge my emotions
Making my hazy life
Visible.

THE VOICE

Pained and pale
My heart shrinks—
Its rosy hue seeps away.

The nourishment for body and soul
Doesn't arrive because no one sees me.
And yet I hear the sound of a voice
No more than a weak moan.
Is that voice mine?...

I am like the cactus in a barren land,
The creeping vegetation of ruins.
The liquid I drink has the bitter taste
Of sour wine.

Because of your absence, which exacts
A harsh price,
My days are like falling stars.
The world has become to me
One devoid of feelings.

WITHOUT VANITIES

I dressed to leave.
I adjusted the folds of the robe
That hung from my shoulders.

From the solitude of my room
I sensed that darkness was approaching.
Shadows invaded my house
And the whole world.

If I ventured
To the only square of Beit She'an
I would be in time to find the end of the afternoon
Bathed in the pallor of the disappearing day;
Inside my abode I got confused
By the short days and the long nights.

I strode from the heavy door
And stepped on stony ground.
Far off I saw appear,
On the top of the mountains,
The groves gleaming in the twilight.
Those who dared to proceed toward
The fortress tower in the besieged city
Would come face to face with the empire of the dark night
And its ghosts.

I returned to my room, removing my delicate garments.
With no dreams or vanities to cover me
I lay on the hard, cold ground, and
Uttered the lament for freedom outside the walls.

FLOW

The contrast
Between the tiny earthly paradise,
Which for a long time I dressed,
And the vastness of the world,
Paralyzes me.

My time flows slowly
In a vacuum
Although reality
Marches toward me:
He who cares for my garden—
Inside other concentric gardens—
Indicating what is beyond
Our own condition.
That which is symbolic
But woven into our bodies
When we breathe,
Eat, sleep,
In an eternal flow
That pushes death
One step ahead.

The overflowing smothers me.
Encircled by the sea,
Sand, and wind,
I exchange my soul
For every and any natural element
That resists human necessities.
I double over
Like the hanged man.

LIGHT

Atop the diagonal stretch
Of forest,
Under the slanting light,
That filters through the vegetation,
On aimless walks
Amidst the shouts of nature
In the gestures that wither
In a sunken idealism
When reality
Rises to our reach,
The extraordinary
Always happens:
The idyllic dream
Unreflected
In boundless space
When a crimson and mysterious form
Languidly sinks its inescapable,
Merciful claws
And momentarily rescues—
The man I am:
Solitary, wandering spirit.

BEYOND THE BORDER

We are tinged
With that unrivaled brilliance
That colors the purest idealism,
Unconditional love,
A feeling that blossoms
More than any other
In our life, split by an ocean.

Without ephemeral dreams, and yet
With serenity manifest
In thought and memory,
Reduced as we are
To our physical limitations,
To hard labor.

Without ephemeral dreams, and yet
With serenity reflected
In the infinite passage of time
Undulating above humanity,
Confusing us,
Penetrating our bodies
Like silver bullets.

DIVE

If I could believe
In the transformation
That comes
By ascending one more step
On the ladder that connects the lowest floor
To the highest heaven,
I would be free
From useless questionings
About time and matter.
I would sense that everything is part
Of the human chain
Of meetings and misses,
Affective surrenders
And excruciating isolations.

They did not see me arrive.
I circulated between the presents.
I transpired an ocean of tensions.

I avoided their gazes
Because I didn't possess
Maturity
Unerring judgment,
Because I didn't know
How to steadily,
Gracefully cross
The moments that form
The whole, indivisible sequence
They call life.

Impotent,
I jumped ship,
I threw myself into the sea
I kept within my soul that which is mine alone.

NORTH

I am terribly tired.
As the days go by, the force of will
That pushes me forward
Slips away.

I have walked about the world. I felt triumphant.
I have sat in the grass and wished for the mountain.
Lying on the sand,
The watery mirror reflecting brilliant gold,
I wished to possess.

Today, tired,
I can't pinpoint the feeling harassing me;
Whether it is absence that cuts at me or
A deeper comprehension of solitude,
Where, by fate, we live…

It is difficult for me to believe in tenderness
But I relent.
I will be waiting in this house
Musty from the sea breeze
With infestations lurking
In the corners.
At this time of withdrawal and forgiveness,
Longing does not grieve me.

In fact, it is memories
Of the time in which the children
Were near
That point me north,
And give meaning to the wait.

THE SAME

It's the night before the party
And it's been a year since I've seen you.
You've forgotten, perhaps, where I live…

My house
Is more hidden away each day.
The vegetation grows around it
And there is no one to prune it for me.

Time passes in a slow,
Murky way,
Implacable—
No one comes to my door anymore
At dawn.

If you wish to save me
From the pain I keep inside
Do not say a single word
It would be useless now.

Only receive my exhausted embrace
My mute prayer and forget-me-not.

I've been punished enough
I could be dead
And it would be the same.

LITTLE DEITY

Son, you are freer
Than I ever dreamed was possible.
Precocious maturity and unbounding courage
Sculpted your reserved disposition,
Solid like a rock,
Often leaving me in awe.

And like two little gods,
Two cats, with a sweetness no human possesses
Have walked by your side with infinite tenderness during the last decade.

The hour has come for Doggy
—the erstwhile spirited cat,
He is close to leaving this world.
His energy seeps away before our eyes.
His meows have become inaudible.
His bones poke through his thin fur.
He weighs less than six pounds…

The doctor asks you to put him in your lap.
You cuddle with him one last time.
She administers the injection.
Old Doggy deflates like a balloon
And sleeps forever.

Our grief materializes in remembering the places
Where he silently crept
Leaving his marks like the master of his own destiny.
The Cat, who so often saves us from ignorance and from the abyss.
Ah, the little deaths are the most touching.

MELINDA'S SECRET

Melinda is alone.
She floats with her four paws
That barely touch the ground.

Without understanding what happened,
She frantically seeks her companion—
In her despair
She runs away from home, her one familiar shelter.
She hopes to find him
Out there in the world.
She follows the path
Of a remote time,
More remote than the Orient,
Bigger than the remotest remembrance.

Melinda is alone.
The house, the yard, the rocks
The blanket with his hairs
The smell of fish
Cannot deliver her from so much pain.

No one saw her slip through the door.
No man dared to prevent her escape.
But there is no one to comfort her anywhere.
Coming back home is a marvelous return.

Melinda is alone.
Never mind that her fur grows
Rapidly and with a good sheen after her return.
No one knows what she sees,
What secret she hides.
The mystery is hers.

OUR FARM

The children led the little colt
Haltingly through the bushes
Back to the stable
Where it found the fresh water
We brought for it to drink
Freely.

All around, the extensive
Grass, well maintained,
Free from blemishes in its greenness
Covered the field
That wafted the smell of the pine trees.

It wasn't fully night yet
But the moon appeared
Static in the sky,
Illuminating our blessed,
Fertile farm.

From Leo, I recited to the children:
… but alone / there is this moon in the sky
that no one ever saw fall except in dreams.

We all looked on in rapture.

CARESSES

In contemplating a reality
That is inscribed somewhere,
I will plunge.
Everything will seem to fit
Into concentric circles,
Spilling over within my eyes
I'll have the feeling
That the world is perfect.

We'll all be together
Walking in the humid,
Aromatic grass,
Recently showered by fine rain.
The clouds in the sky
Will send their caresses
Which we'll make into our pillows,
They'll be so close—
We'll need only to extend our arms
To glean a little piece of them.
We, our children, and their children.

MAY YOU BE WELCOME

Your name shines
On the work I sculpted in marble,
On the bronze gate of my house
And on the sign on which I wrote:
May you be welcome.

You who were born
In the Promised Land
Called Israel,
From there you migrated, little one
With golden curls on your head
To Terra Brasilis
Where you grew shrouded in mystery,
When the curls transformed
Into a beautiful sunny day
Full of virtues and feelings.

For a long time, now,
You've lived in the North,
Rich and far away.
You are sublime like the date palm,
From which your name is derived:
A tree which produces fruit for a hundred years
And, because it is straight, tall and imposing
Became a symbol of the perfect man.

DROWNING

Take me
Closer to you
Take me
To the beginning of everything
When you were so small,
Fragile and endearing,
That I can only mourn bitterly
The memory of a time that doesn't return,
The feelings I could not express entirely
In those moments and places
Of memory that lasts a lifetime.

Take me
Quickly, unhesitatingly
So I don't die,
So I can seek forgiveness
Purge away the infinite sadness,
The remorse that never runs out
Because it's irrational, diffuse
And soon will drown me
In the watery, salty torrent
Of tears that fall copiously.

OCEAN OF TIME

An ocean of time
Separating us,
An indescribable nostalgia
Filling my days.

The pressing need
To be present, body and soul,
In the small and unadorned abode
Where you live.

The urge to share
In your laugh and your grief,
Your sustenance,
The unwinding of your activities
Between each foreseeable moment.

The desire to infiltrate myself gently
Into the unimaginable,
With permission,
For I don't know how to invade another's space.

Everything convulses me
In the filthy, lonely alleyway
Where I live and where I'll die
On a beautiful, bright day.
Amen.

REST

On the bright afternoons
At October's end
In Har Haguilboa
The pure air magnifies
The transparent sounds
That rise from the valley.
The song of the birds
And the groan of the wind
Sound like an idyllic manifestation
Of nature at rest.

You see the turf, Ben,
Covered in dry leaves,
It's a carpet colored
With your unique design
Which will be short lived.

At the end of the season that's coming
The carpet will be no more.
The leaves will have died into the earth
A silent and hidden death
Whose secret we will never live to know.

UTOPIA

I was everything and I am nothing.
I cling to a recurring dream,
An idyllic utopia,
That comforts me again and again;
Restarting life,
Inhabiting this life.

I lived on the corners
I learned to release into the air
Words that devoured my soul.
From there I went to the center,
To the core of existence,
Where we find ourselves
Spilling forth our instincts over and over,
But this only proved my inability
To captivate and make myself hear.

I went back to the edges of reality
And with each new day I think;
It's not so bad to wake up,
To set the table in the garden;
Who knows, maybe someone will come by
Accompanied by crickets and butterflies;
Who knows, maybe someone will appear
Like a sprout from the earth:
Hallucinate me with the wonder of the never-pondered.

On second thought, all that isn't necessary
The secret gesture of tenderness,
Which I learned not to rely on,
Is enough to burst the dike
Of what I dam up inside.

MIRAGE

You're alone, Ben.
You seek answers
Following revelations
That only to an eligible few—
Such as the wise
Who interpreted the mystic Kabbalah—
Is given to understand.

You seek answers
In the cold environment that surrounds you
Amidst the cold algorithms and symbols
That multiply, divide,
Perform countless operations
So that a shallow equilibrium
Flows through the chaos of the universe.

At this same time in which, disoriented,
Flushed with shame,
I search for words to translate the aridity of existence.

I walk unprotected over burning rocks
Consuming my soul
With so much worrying and wandering
Under the blazing heat
Where I drag my feet, my body,
Until I make out a green oasis
That I never reach
Without your company.

CATHARSIS

My nature
Is the absence of your nature.
I am a burning body
Sculpted by desire
A rough diamond
Set by hopelessness,
By an emptiness so vast
that with its antitheses
It fills me to the brim.

You are he
Who contains in himself
All the time in the world.
You are he
To whom sleep comes quickly.
And the anxieties,
The urgency of life
Evaporate before they reach you.

In full madness
My voiceless cry explodes:
"Save me from isolation!"

MATURING

All my life
I'll remember the day
In which your unique, immaculate
Profile,
Intimated an ineffable elixir.

The unexplainable day
In which your voice fit
More harmoniously into a verse
Shaped by the finest of substances:
The language of men,
Than into the universe of thick matter
That rips from us our innocence.

Your magnified being,
Ennobled
By bowing to fate
Lost from its own identity
Seemed to nourish me
From far away.

Under words proffered
As if in a prophecy to the heart,
Under the effect of proximity,
At the touch of our hands,
We matured.
We transformed cold absence
Into warm presence—
We rescued each other.

LOVE

Ah, if I love you...
I let you direct me
Along the paths.
I am exhilarated always
By the wind
That comes from the sea
And arrives at the waterfront we walk
At the cross streets
We use to walk back.

We share the same view
The same truth about the world
We examine the well-kept flower beds
And the trees that reach
The tallest buildings.

Ah, if I love you...
Lead me with your soft, decisive step
Take me into an embrace that's enveloping
Like the brightness of a brisk morning.
I surrender myself to you,
Who asks nothing
And is always present:
You cover me when I am cold,
You comfort me after nightmares.

Together we are
Happiness.

IMMINENCE

I lived beauty on high.
On the imposing summit
I transcended life on the plain.
As the water from the spring disappeared
It pacified one of the cardinal points
Of my ancestral thirst.
The bush that flourished
On the rugged rock
Cast rejuvenating shade over me.
The low sky,
The brilliance of the king star
That bade farewell
Enveloped me in the mantle
Of religiousness
And brought me the elegy
That made the fleeting
Moment eternal.
The reflection in the mirror
Brought that spring of crystal waters
That I reclaimed
Inside a secret submerged forest
In my soul, pacified
By some unknown deity.

ELEGY

Hidden under the vegetation
The white spring
With drops of aged gold
No longer outpours its pure waters.
But it contains inside
Like the portico of an ancient palace
The feeling of a sad refrain
Spilled over the world.

In it one can spy,
Magnificently superimposed,
The Great Temple of Jerusalem
The Wailing Wall
And all the cathedrals.

In it one can find the path
To go back and forth in time.
In front of it there has always been the bush,
Where, in the desert,
Moses heard the voice of God.

Such immense silence and harmony
Forged a path there.
If water flowed from it
One could gather in hand
All the flux of existence.

CRACK IN THE SOUL

To my great joy
The trees sway
With their branches close to the window.
In synchrony with the reflections of the sun
And the constant breeze
They move like a golden pendulum.

I can close my eyes
To engrave in my soul
Their verdant, crystal beauty.
When I return to look at them
They'll be in the same place
In their continual movement.

Nothing can bring me
More peace at this moment.

The day is glorious
The expanse beyond the trees
Overflows from the horizon,
Opens a crack in the soul
So that the sensation
Of synchrony and completeness
With the world outside
Penetrates this fissure that opened up
In my minuscule universe.

ED

The heart celebrates tenderly.
It dances on the fringes
That mingle in the days that roll on.

The crumbs are on the table.
The cups, with their water evaporating.

On the sofa the cat sleeps
The sleep of the just.

Present and future blend together:
They give shape to a lake of placid, crystal waters.

Today is Ed's birthday
The heart celebrates with a pang
Between two realities that interweave.

Fany Aktinol

CALIFORNIA, SUMMER 2012

The horizon is flat
Without projections or mountains
No clouds are in the sky
The sun's blaze shines in 360 degrees.

A superhuman heat
Pours over bodies
During the endless days of summer.

The impalpable, secret desire,
The supreme passion for life that burns
And offers itself in its glory
Represents a promise of happiness
Within reach of my hand.

The dimming of another long day arrives:
The circle of fire will gently dive
Into the earth
Crinkling with its reflections
The linear landscape
Entirely tinged by the blood-red.

I will tremble imperceptibly
Before the tremendous sight and
My mouth will pronounce the fleeting moment
In a whisper:
Ah, God, how to stand such beauty?

THE MOTHER

Poetry is a scar
And also dew.
Blue sky. Tall mountains.
Deep seas. Rivers that flow.
To write is to drink of spring water.
Soothe the distressed spirit and
With a bare breast receive the cold wind.
It is to find oneself on the way home.
To recognize oneself in the arrow shot forth.

You have arrived, distant son.
Since then spring
Reigns in every corner
With the blossoming of the most tender flowers,
With the warm breeze
And its breath of pure rapture.

With your departure near,
Once more,
The memory of golden days
Strikes me like a lightning bolt:
No one on this earth
Except our mother
Deserves so much pain
And so many scars.

LEGACY

From the high mountains
To the soft and verdant plains
The home of free men, she descended.
Above the eyes, scars—
Marks from the sun, from the rains,
And from the stars.

Come down, it's time.
She listened among the noise of the wind.
The mother came before with the child
From exile to the new land
To the school of life.

The context and the circumstance:
The mother arrived with the little one
With little money,
Little bread and little clothing,
And as for tenderness, overflowing.
The outcome, the true and
Impalpable inheritance.

FINAL DESTINATION

We strip ourselves
Of any shred of self-esteem
In the melancholy abyss of the days.
From nostalgia to nostalgia
We reach the lowest levels
Of hopelessness.
What is solid and stable
Frays.
The concept of normalcy,
Of the most banal human habits, evaporates.
I feel strangely close
To individuals on the margins of society.

I love you, distant children.
My time is short.
I must go.
I have a feeling that the train
Has arrived at its last platform.

LOVE WAITS

The time I measure
No longer in days or months,
But in years,
The distance measured
Not by cities or countries,
But by continents,
Leave marks that lash
Like a sandstorm.

For lack of courage
I did not yield to despair
I can be happy
In the most unlikely moments.
I mask my pain
—everything hurts, and so nothing hurts anymore.
And sometimes life seems to make sense
As it does now, Ben.

Love always waits.
Under this circumstance
Days gone by fade away
And those that belong to the future
Shine.

ABSENCE

My life,
My minuscule, immaculate
Work—
If I take into account
My illuminated descendants,
That slide along freely—
Is a work of sand,
Inconclusive.
My hands are covered in the dust
Of endless epiphanies
Of all there is to do, build,
Express with a cry
Smothered in my throat.

The impossibility of accomplishing it,
Makes it more pressing,
Indispensable like the air.
Through some inherited mystery
The sense of humanity
Never leaves me
It makes me reverent, vulnerable,
And by the force of destiny,
My savage ego,
My words,
Soon will be little more
Than smudges
Dissolved in the sand
And washed by sea water.

NAVIGATING

It was a moment
Etched with eternity,
Unfathomable.
I looked with admiration at the sun
Plowing the thick water
In the direction of an imaginary island.

Reflected on the twilight seas
The sunset threw sideways
Its dying rays of sunshine.

I hesitated.
The light still shone
Above my head.
In the unending sequence of thoughts
I felt indestructible—
The words of a philosopher-king aided me:
I will love you and do good to you,
Though you may not know it.

But in that infinite moment
The transfigured sea
Called me to rest in its peace
To make the ultimate journey,
To sail the sea of life.

TANNENBAUM

You reflect the perfumed pine
When you give it form
In an image
Like a living spine
Filled to the brim
With resplendent verdure
And within,
In the half light,
The stalk of the arteries
Flows in the direction
Of its beating nucleus.

You can eternalize it in a name,
Reproduce it,
Transmit its nature
Until in a sacred, secret
Instant,
Its force,
Its magnetism
Overcome you
Giving shape
To a delicate
And cohesive unity,
Constituting your essence
All life long.

Fany Aktinol

MATTER OF LIFE

Life is always excessive
In the imperceptible sliding of the days.
In a single day
Fit the mysteries of philosophy,
Of metaphysics,
Of the Essenes—
Whose secret was knowing how to deal with silence.
But words—representation of the real,
Are the matter of life.

Sandra, exhibit her pictures in the gallery.
Her theme is grand, atemporal,
It finds a balance
Between the smoothness of the traces
And the natural beauty of the trees she paints,
Of the great trunks that are born from the earth
And grow heavenward
As if they were alive.

On a stretch of clear sky
She writes, with clear and delicate brushstrokes,
A poem of my own making.
I seek an explanation, a divine link
For the sublime connection that exists in us,
For the chain of events
That occur throughout life.
But there is nothing to seek,
The secret is before me.
The representation of the real is all there is.

REFUGE

Binjamin,
To what land will we escape
After the life-breaking tempest?
The cry of the heavens
Comes in the flash of lightning
In the clap of thunder.
They ignite the assembly-path
That cuts through the city
And with its hand
Gathers each living creature.

The entire coast is swept,
What is delicate and fragile,
A flower, a small animal,
Disappears from view, swallowed by the flood.
All that remains is dead-living nature
That floats like Chagall's figures.

The shock points to the face of God
Which lights up tragically.
It casts fear into the soul.
No one goes from one side to another
Because there are no longer sides.
The city has transformed
Into a lake with limitless reach
Of saturated earth
Feverishly illuminated
Shaken by the sound
That breaks its last barrier.

And it's a miracle we survived
Until this day in which truth
Can no longer be found
Because it lives in the heights.

SEDIMENTS

The urgency in writing
The acrostic with your name,
The epic poem
Of your immense and glorious history,
Agitates me like the wind
That blows without relief.

I am the tree that shakes
Its branches,
I am the innumerable leaves
That fall to the earth
Imprinting the perfect painting
Sedimented over time.

My words
Charged with nostalgia and melancholy
Are the leaves that fall to the ground
Like emotional tears.

My words are for you
And for whoever else
Would like to give them the meaning
That time strengthened.

Fany Aktinol

THE DAYS

Subtle
Are the rare moments
Of pure liberty
And release
When we can do everything—
We intuit a universe
To our liking.

An old, dilapidated carousel
Drowns us in a sea of horses
That, in their gentle madness,
Spin our idle thoughts.

Above us only the blue sky,
Only the throbbing doubt:
Why should we move upon the Earth,
Count the days, the years
—Why should we measure time—
If not to prove our survival
In planetary solitude…

I see myself prone, embracing this Earth,
Only the sky, the air,
Its smells, sounds
Enveloping me, consoling me,
Making me tremble
Until the last of my days.

Fany Aktinol

THE RABBIS SING

It still blows
The wind that passed over the valley of bones
In Ezekiel's vision
Giving life to the remains
Of those who had long since died.

I wished to learn the prayers
Even though I lacked the essential faith.
I wished to learn them
Because of their coherence, which guides me—
Even in the valley of the lost, I bowed down.
I wished to learn them
Because of the coherence imprinted in my spirit
Through the legacy I received.

I am drawn to the songs
Of the Day of Forgiveness
Sung by the six rabbis
In the Great Temple.
I am elated and go to the heavens
The voices are sublime like Handel's music.
They make flesh arise from the remains.

MEMORIES

The weight of a name
The rustle of steps
The painful groans
Of the decaying boards.

The absent, paralyzing
Immensity of the world.
The simultaneous existence
Of memory and forgetting.
The atemporal melody
Of wind in the house on the hills,
In the temple of the sacred books,
Of the goblets of wine,
Of the cider and of the pomegranate.

The key that opens the door
Of our circular passion
Birth, growth, death.

And all that no longer will be—
Like God
Without our presence.

REQUIEM

We are light in the midst of deep shadows.
We celebrate with a requiem—
Not death—
But rebirth.

When we meet again
I realize how much I love all around me.
Which makes life something sacred.
I feel also that nothing
That was done until now
Is comparable to what will yet be done.

Art is long, life is short.
Illuminated are the words of the courageous,
Heroic are their acts,
Of those that plow ahead,
And read the Soul:
Our lives are the unending river
Built from meetings and separations.

To that end we brave the current
And keep the flame of existence burning,
That which runs over the bed of stones—
Because we risk forfeiting rebirth
Unless we cross it.

SHORTCUT

In this strange life at a distance
Which we never even dreamed of,
And which fate offered us,
We must let ourselves be enchanted like the serpent,
Migrate like the swallow,
Be light and agile like the hummingbird.

We must know of the inverted seasons.
Scorching summer in this burning land
In the other, permafrost—winter of frozen ground.

Flowering spring in the southern hemisphere
In the north, autumn with its fallen leaves.

I am alone, contemplating from the high heaven,
And, at other times, from the deepest ocean,
The hours that give meaning to everything.
It will never be different
Nor better than this passage
Allotted to us now.

TO WHOM?

May I not have lost my way
In the absent immensity of the universe,
In forgetting,
In the atemporal melody
Of exuberant nature
Or of the temples in ruins.

May I not have gotten confused
In the empty days
Dissecting the contradictions
So fundamentally impressed on me.

May I not have been led astray
By promises
Of vibrant and bright days,
Of adventures without beginning or end
From sunrise to sunset.

Behold here, with its implacable presence,
Fate,
Offering me the abyss:
A fissure that opens in my soul.

I wish for solitude
Total and absolute
And I wish to possess nothing,
Not brilliant matter,
Nor ethereal philosophy.

My malady is inscrutable

And I ask myself with the shred of will that remains
Who will benefit
From receiving what flows through me—
Through my stubbornly warm body?
I must transmit
Some spark of passion and madness
To someone…
But to whom, Venerable Lady?
To whom?

AT A GALLOP

When in the pallid afternoons
Of shifting brightness
You venture out
In a sea of uninterrupted words
That gush forth like cascading water,
When you cannot find the time
To listen to your neighbor,
I feel my own loneliness:
You see all beings, Immanuel,
With imprecise contours,
Traced in your image.

Can you imagine violent passion
Or profound pain, as the day goes by?
I walk atop a bed of stones
With no one to cling to.

Wishing for night to come
Because day means being eternally adrift,
Dissembling and torturing oneself
With the one who is nearby,
The other who is distant,
And the universe as a whole,
For which I am imperfect.
Desiring to leave the body
Inhabit spaces
Is my secret desire
Renewed day by day.

In the course of life

—may God grant that it not be long—
The visionary amalgam will form
From squalor and compassion
That will come at a gallop
And I'll absorb it
Addicted as I am to such suffering.

I

With no thought for the return
Ecstasy erupts
Like rain in the desert.
It blossoms in a flood
Whose touch is ever so soft,
Redemptive,
In the convulsive beauty
Of latent emotions.

Despite the inverted seasons,
The lateness of the hour,
I give myself to you
For brief, impermanent days
And ephemeral moments of passion
When we plunge
Into unthinkable confidences
That I preserve tenaciously,
Without tempering them.
I,
Who came from so far.

SPROUTING

I am like the white, withering light,
That in this world has only the clear sun.
I imbibed the sap of the field, the aroma of the fertile
earth
And I stumbled,
I lost consciousness—
I wished to rest there for eternity.

If it weren't for a messenger
Who came from the beyond
And whispered in my ear:
– Arise and walk among the sharp thorns,
Cross the muddy swamps…,
I wouldn't have noticed a spark reflected in the sky
Sending me its flashes.
I arose with peace in the spirit,
I sprouted like the golden stalk of wheat,
And arrived in time to eat the bread.

DISPOSABLE

It will always be summer somewhere,
And I learn that it's possible to die,
Between two summers.

I will be far
From the truth I know,
Close to an existence
Without memories or hopes,
Affections or familiar sounds,
Without tangible or comprehensible values.

Only apocryphal stories
Will come to my mind
In a time in which
Reflections in the atmosphere—pallid,
Blueish, cold—
Will make me tremble
From the savage root
I planted one day
In the deep and fertile earth.
So that from that spot
It could grow among the elements
Until the final hour.

GRAVESTONE

I touched the stone. I felt myself inside eternity.
And in one moment, I was moved
By the spark of my ancestors:
A carved message
That my fingers deciphered
Pushing me toward a sweet, lyrical strain.

Standing, I shrunk behind the marble stone
Of the grave of my parents.
I wept silently,
I asked without feeling worthy:
"Protect me from the detours and the falls,"
In these powerful, sacred moments
In which they flow in my blood.

I stroked the rock—History in itself.
That which is in the world as I am
Contains the secret of creation,
For I am just a passenger.
But I wish to see beyond the mystery,
I wish to hear its beating heart
Inside the universe.

PSALM

May my prayer
Be stronger
Than my feeble faith and understanding.
May the illusion disappear,
The vain futility,
Taking with it the anxieties that consume me.

I wish to sing the psalm of love
So I can give more unconditional love
Without the lament of a drowning heart.

May transcendence be stronger than longing
So I can dive
In the placid waters of the ocean
Without the lament of my drowning heart.

I carry with me universal passion
Never totally transmitted,
Because once I submerged
I never again recovered.

FESTIVAL OF LIGHTS

During Hanukkah—the Festival of Lights,
Candles burn for eight days
In the eight-armed candelabra—
Always close to a window—
So they can be seen
By those outside the house.

Illuminating the darkness that exists in the world
Is a commandment of this festival.
The candle, with its burning flame,
Symbolizes a human being:
The wax represents the body
And the light—the soul.

In my house
Candles were always lit
In a sacred ritual never forgotten.
The faith I lack
My parents had to spare.
And the spiritual greatness,
Ah, I will never have their greatness.

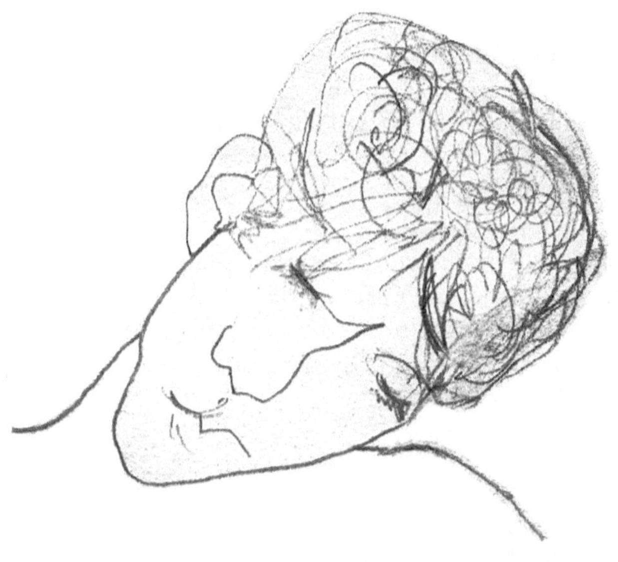

Fany Aktinol

THE NEIGHBOR

Upstairs
Lives an old lady
With blue eyes and silky skin.

Even before the morning broke
Her caretaker dragged her feet and the furniture
Over my head.

I implored for silence
In those hours in which the world sleeps.
But she disavowed any and all sounds,
And each of my pleadings.

On a tempestuous day
Of intense wind, lightning and thunder,
Her window came loose and flew away.
The ground smoldered. There was affliction upstairs,
As if in a manifestation of the wrath
Of He who lives on high…

Peace and silence mysteriously returned.
Her now-rare footsteps, and diffused sounds,
Make me tremble,
They still prowl around and invade my dreams
Along with the thunderous peals of the storm.

Today I ran into her,
The old lady with her caretaker.
Her eyes were even more blue,
Her skin even more silky.
We greeted each other cordially
As if the recent past had never happened.

LAP

The night
Delays its coming.
The morning
delays its birth.
The days are swept away
The slower the pace
The larger the loss.

I know that you are wind,
Craggy rock,
Stormy thunder:
Supreme nature—
Oh, incalculable nostalgias.

I know that I am what I've lost.
The reflection in my countenance
Is inconsolable,
Bitterly agitated.
The slow sunset
Is my image that is extinguished
And plows ahead with broad steps
Toward the eternity
That has already prepared its lap
For me.
My soul lights up.
The end of all pain is near.

FALL

For a swan
Perfectly beautiful
Immaculate to the extreme
Gracefully formed
Surrounded by a magical, immanent
Aura,
I shed large tears
That the torrent transforms
Into a pebble
And I am
In the smallest contours
Before my wondering eyes
A defenseless creature
Due to some commotion
At the dawn of life
That made my heart bleed
Transforming me into the alter ego
Of the lofty swan—
A cataclysm of nature.

THE UNKNOWN

At eight o'clock in the morning
Every day
The indefatigable man from Akko
Shows up to work.

I see him from my window—
This small portal
To a prison with no walls—
Carrying fruit and vegetables,
In an incessant coming-and-going,
Of the endless chain
Of greens, figs,
Dates, apricots…

Solitarily, remotely,
Many meters away,
I contemplate him tenderly
And because we are in a vast plain,
I have a dense,
Strangely intimate view,
Without obstacles,
Of his poignant figure.

Sitting at my window
In hypnotic observation
I am emotionally touched,
In a moving way,
By this stranger
Who doesn't even know I exist.

EXCEPT FOR ME

I am the expatriate
Distant as if in another world.
I feel life burning,
Boiling, volatile,
Facing me
Rooted in a slow fire
Of sleepless eyes.

I am the expatriate
Of the limitless beyond,
Of indistinguishable lands and oceans.
I want to sleep and forget
Slowly, secretly,
That I was not granted
Equilibrium
Although I can see it
On the line of the horizon
That cuts through sky and ocean,
In the tall mountains,
In the flight of a bird,
In the humid, verdant land,
In the most tender flower that grows.
Except for me, everything is harmony.

IMPONDERABLE

I heard when you said:
"I am one hundred percent materialist."
But I tell myself:
"Look how you come closer, overcoming the improbable.
You are also one hundred percent
The quintessence of human commotion."

Otherwise, how can you explain
The extensive attributes,
The instantaneous comprehension and interaction
With your neighbor,
Your tender and latent lyricism?

How can one understand your irreprehensible
cheerfulness,
Your personal exuberance in communication,
When often, as you say nothing,
You say everything.

How can one decipher your detachment
Your unparalleled commitment
That entrances the most naïve
And confuses the most extravagant?

You are the figurehead—
Despite the distance—
Of my life, precarious and fluid,
That will be by my side to unchain me.

FUTURE

Today I won't go to the beach alone—
The path is short,
I walk two blocks to step onto the sand.

Today I lie down on a corner of the bed
From which I can see the deep blue of the sky
Which hypnotizes me for just a few seconds.
Soon my eyelids close.
Its light hurts the eyes.

To go to the beach is to approach the kingdom of the sun.
A ritual that repeats itself during the summers of life:
The front door that I open,
The elevator that takes me to the ground floor,
The sidewalks and the streets that I cross
Until I reach the sand and the salty water.

The most banal things are
Those that will remain for centuries to come.
The smooth asphalt of the streets,
The sidewalks made from little stones
The sea breeze that invades the atmosphere
They will never know
When I am no longer
Here to walk along them.

SANDY HOOK

The children sing
The first songs of the day
They plant the morning flowers.
And inexplicable insanity
Blooms.
The delirium that comes through guns
Makes us hallucinate in the darkest hour
In the hand that pulls the trigger
To kill the purest innocence:
Children that sang songs in the morning—
Will never sing again
Because their voices were stolen forever,
Their entire life was cut down
Forever.

Mystery is all around us:
Waves that break
Endlessly
Do not spoil
Or corrupt
Or make us bleed
Or succumb to the maelstrom
Despite the feverish activity—
Despite the continual blows on the fine sand—
They echo only sublime beauty
In the thunderous breakers
With their pure white foam.

How this astonishes me!
Blows transformed into a maritime symphony.

Today I only wish to be close
To this primitive bliss,
To this eternal chant of nature
That hides nothing from me
And reveals everything:
The little beings
Arrived at the world above.
From there, who knows,
They may continue reciting their nursery rhymes…

A PRAYER

In the Zohar,
The most important compilation
Of Kabbalah,
Jerusalem is situated at the center of the universe,
Hanging over the great abyss,
The "tehom" where the cosmos were created.

Jerusalem, give us peace,
Save us from war,
Hear the prayers
Of those who depart, of those who stay.
Suffering is a twisted circle.

Golden Jerusalem,
Hear the messages that choke
Each crack in the Wailing Wall
And that, murmured, saturate the atmosphere
From dawn to dusk
In a millenarian movement.

I, who never knew the reach of a plea
Write this almost superhuman prayer
That I don't understand with reasoning,
But only with the heart.

It is written
Without my knowing
What is permissible to ask
And what is already inscribed
In the designs of the universe.

THIN SHELL

Lost in the green expanse
Of the infinite ocean
When seen from space
Man thinks himself god.
He resists the sirens' call:
And his own hallucinations.

But the slow passage of the hours
Overtakes him after he has shed his divinity.
Terrified
He feels the lash of the waves
Against his vessel.
A thin shell, humid and fractured
Separates him from the angry water
Where he wanders alone
At the whim of the incessant wind.

His fate as a helpless living being
Ebbs and flows inside me
As if we dreamed the same dreams.

This man carries in himself all men.
He is a symbol of all humanity.

Humanity that
In moments of imminent shipwreck
Only feels the flow of their own blood
In their veins.
To live is not banal nor fleeting.

LIKE THE DIAMOND

I have been to Antwerp,
Land of diamonds and suicides.
I came back whole and pieced
Together the fragments of my soul.

The wisdom of Leo taught me
The unforgettable,
That which really matters,
Dreams, the pliable philosophy of life,
The joy that always conquers
At the end of the journey.

No story
Is more melancholy or withdrawn,
More paradoxically replete with sun
And moments of pure happiness,
Than mine.

Ben,
I am hard and transparent
Like the diamond.
I want to go, but I can't,
I don't break so easily.
And I suffer from the rigidity
Of my senses.

What destiny awaits
The tall mountains,
The infinite sky and sea,
My absurd anxiety
For life?

FRAGMENTS

Framed
By the long-off brightness
In its blinding outline
We compose an unintelligible
Dimension.

Our eyes
Are fragmented into a thousand colors
They drag a chain
Of mystery and dreams
They hear the echo of the music—
The murmur of the wind in the air
Cries of birds—
That come from the barren plain.

We are trailblazers
Of a hidden world
Of an invisible cathedral
Where the link was sculpted
Between those who arrive
And those who leave.

SCAR

I will learn to reign in my world
As one who breathes delicately,
With an open door to those who come—
With their sounds and words,
With compassion for the ragged lives
Of each one of us—
Always, always reinventing myself.

But the other, with permanent scars,
Will persist
Until the twilight of days falls.
She will insist on tearing light from stones and
From her internal cavern.

Beethoven will flood her with soft grief
Spinoza will console her
With the humanism of his philosophy.

However, she will taste
The bitter flavor of defeat,
Of the absence of horizons.
She will hope that fate will grant her
A dubious grace,
A merciful act,
Both paradoxical and fatal—
The bullet shattering the future
Into a thousand fragments.
Because life is incurable.

CANTICLE

The old soldier mounted his steed.
Pieces of iron armor covered him,
Weighing down his still-upright body.

From inside his helmet he gave the order to advance:
The trumpets sounded
And the soldiers raised their voices
In a war chant—
The whole world was shaken.

His calloused heart beat quickly,
The view of the high city to the west was clouded,
The silence was broken with violence
When the shofar sounded.

Yochanan played his cymbals
That reverberated through the open space
And above the rest
Boomed the Levites' song:
Great is the Lord in the Mountain of His Holiness.

The men went to war
Against the numerous enemy.
The victories were great
Because the people of Judah did not bow
To other gods.

In this way, I believe, some
Of the moments of History occurred
In the time of the Maccabees.

STRAND OF LIFE

The world is multiple,
Inconstant and illusory
For the common man.
But in its irreducibility
No temple
Will remain standing
Without human existence.

Leaning on this parapet
Of hanging white stones
Touched millennia ago
By the patriarchs Abraham, Isaac, and Jacob
I digress.

Distant from any rationalization
Without any human contact
I have this cruel impression
Of the future:
In some prosaic moment
Of dispassionate maturity
Perpetually on the margins of society
In tandem with my repressed emotions
I shall witness
In all their insignificance
The mystery of life,
The enigma of the sphynx.

I will pour forth with meaningless words
The chaotic sound
Of a world that collapses

Without its temples,
Without its street corners
Hemming up the strand of life.

MERCY

If this were a biblical time
There would be a man
Of Moses's stature in his generation.

You can envision it, Yasmin.
The multitude concentrated
In a compact mass
To hear him outside the temple.
The man of the field whose only possession
Was the staff on which he leaned.
As an interlocutor with God
Requesting rain for the desert.
With his mouth that moved
In this intimate and universal prayer
In a primitive plea.

You can envision him in his solitude:
In the moment when an unexpected cold wind blew
Followed by other gusts.
The silent firmament was stirred.
Flocks of clouds flowed
Over the mountain.
Black clouds gathered
In the west.
The whole miracle was imminent.
But the hours passed
And the sky still held back its mercy
Until a long time passed
And the immense torrent descended on the earth.

IRRELEVANCE

Under the charged atmosphere, in somber seas,
In the deranged journeys
Of winding, serpentine trails,
In the impossible phenomena,
Like the spark of God that blinded us,
We renounced the pagan idea
Of slow extinction of any life,
Of the transformation of the world
Into a flat desert—
Only sand,
With no stars in the sky
Or paths in the earth—
In the landscape disguised as death.

Lines from a hallucinated bible
That reveals no secret and announces nothing new,
Transfigures us into irrelevant beings,
Without aspirations, without a place in the future—
Without the life that is never
Where we think it is.

Just the delicacy of silence
And the latent courage that resists,
As voice and conscience are increasingly repressed,
Supporting us at their core.

EXTEMPORANEOUS

The silent music of the body
The desert of men around
Transformed your pain and dissipation
Into an immensely pleasing languor,
Without imperfections—
A crystalline world—
When the sound of a voice inside,
Meek, insinuating,
Revived you
And restored temperance.

But the suggestion was lethal,
This was the voice of Death
Making itself heard—
And in its siren song
With its seductive tone,
Smooth and fatal,
You were almost sucked
Away into a vortex with no return.

You intuited, however, that your time
Had not arrived.
Your hour was yet to come.

Fany Aktinol

PERCEPTION

The last frontier
I was able to reach
Dissolves inside of me.
I no longer recognize myself.
My existence
Is only inferred
Through my poems,
Through the sensibility that sprouts
From its intrinsic, structural
Melody
That separates poetry
From other genres,
As it separates me
So many times
From the entire world.

Who will benefit from poetry—
The wise and absent?
The naïve and present?
All of these:
Those who identify
In the silent rite,
In the cultivation of solitude,
In the magnetic
Strength of disavowal
Of the excessive and superficial.

ANCESTRALITY

I retreat a few steps
To contemplate it entirely—
The tree with its innumerable branches,
That opens like a fan—
And to breathe its millennial fertility.

Its venerable, welcoming posture,
Its smell of remote nature,
Ah, the smell we lost
In the evolutionary process
Makes me resume the rotation
Toward this singular ancestor
Concretely within my reach.

I let myself get carried away, in silence,
With my senses sharpened,
I want to simulate it;
I gently envelop it,
Its texture, its scents,
Eternal, sacred,
They invade me, make me shudder—
They are living extensions
Of the earth's core,
Imperceptible in their ascent
Their sublime adventure
Destined heavenward,
From the earthy soil,
Uterus of every living being.

Fany Aktinol

SOWER OF THE UNIVERSE

Mira is a star
With a long tail.
As it crosses through space
At supersonic speeds
It leaves fragments
Or "seeds" along the way
For new solar systems.

Mira's tail emits oxygen
And other essential elements
For the formation of new stars,
Planets and lives.
Monumental is her capacity to take over
Our imagination and commotion.

The sower of the universe
Is somewhere
In the blue sky
Invisible to our eyes,
In a place lost from view,
In the extraordinary mystery of the cosmos,
Where the distances and the unknown
Are just as powerful as the dense silence.

FANY AKTINOL was born in Rio de Janeiro in 1953. She is a writer and librarian, author of *Um atalho entre o sol e a solidão* [*A shortcut between the sun and solitude*] (prose poetry, Ibis Libris, 2004), *O sol se põe no meu corpo* [*The sun sets on my body*] (poetry, 7Letras, 2009), *O tom da infância* [*The tone of childhood*] (novel, 7Letras, 2010) e *Sob o esplendor de milhares de sóis* [*Under the blaze of thousands of suns*] (poetry, 7Letras, 2014). Currently, Fany lives in California.